THE FIVE CONVERSATIONS OF HIGHLY EFFECTIVE MANAGEMENT TEAMS

How They Anticipate Threats To Achieving Their Objectives And Identify Opportunities To Exploit For A Competitive Advantage

ED KEMPKEY

Find out how your team can make better decisions for better results at:

www.RiskSkillsCenter.com

ISBN-13: 978-1979996907

ISBN-10: 1979996903

ENDORSEMENTS AND ACCOLADES

"Ed brought our team a systematic way to identify, evaluate, rank and mitigate the risks that were present in the ongoing operation of our business. It was one of the best investments of time that we have made at Clos Du Val. I am excited to continue to build upon our expertise in this area as it will positively impact the future of the winery."

Steve Tamburelli, President & CEO,
Clos Du Val Wine Co.

"We have been using Ed's Managing Uncertainty system for two years at the Boys & Girls Clubs of Napa Valley. Not only has it helped provide a framework for our strategic direction, it also highlights what is most important for our organization to achieve success. I would highly recommend this to any organization that desires to establish a reliable basis for decision making and planning in order to achieve their objectives."

Mark Kuhnhausen, Executive Director,
Boys and Girls Clubs of Napa Valley

"Over a 25-year career, I have worked with hundreds of private business owners to increase the financial value of their equity. One of our guiding principles is "Simple Good." Although it sounds straight-forward, it's not easy to

achieve conditions that empower the owner, and teams at all levels, to act decisively when there are more "unknowns" than "knowns." Five Conversations offers many important insights but I cannot overstate the importance of its most crucial contribution: in five completely intuitive steps, it's possible to achieve clarity about uncertainty. Any company that embraces Ed Kempkey's Managing Uncertainty System will undoubtedly make better decisions faster – and enjoy significant and sustainable competitive advantages as a result."

**Sean Hutchinson, Partner,
SVA Value Accelerators**

"It is rare to meet someone as passionate and knowledgeable about reducing risk and uncertainty in business as Ed Kempkey. Uncertainty is accelerating and management teams are being challenged to succeed in today's tumultuous environment. In this book, Ed provides an innovative and experience-based approach for leaders of companies to use in assuring the achievement of their objectives."

Mel Engle, CEO, Engle Strategic Solutions

"My biggest takeaway from the Ed's workshop was that Risk Management is much more than safety. It's taking a good look with your Executive team of all risks the company faces, prioritizing them and putting together a plan to minimize the risk, and then incorporate the plan into your day-to-day business. The ISO 31000 standards we reviewed simplifies this process and makes it easy to implement. I would recommend this to any company as a great tool to manage risk."

Bill Blum, General Manager, MacArthur Place

"I was absolutely amazed that we were able to effectively cover so much ground in a short time. The workshop was very well organized; first laying the foundation and framework of enterprise risk management, and then identification of risks specific to our own individual organizations. This workshop created an awareness of how valuable a comprehensive risk management program can be in helping us achieve our organizational goals. It was impressive to learn that risk management can include opportunities and positive gains and not apply just to mitigating losses. Exposure to the principles, framework, and process of risk management showed how we could improve decision making throughout our organization by using this structured approach. It really sends you away with the sense that we need to start doing this now."

**Peter Stoppello, Board Member,
Boys and Girls Clubs of Napa Valley**

WHY I WROTE THIS BOOK?

Over the span of my forty-plus year career as a commercial insurance broker, I was fortunate to work with many organizations in a variety of industries. This experience provided me the opportunity to observe how management teams make decisions, particularly in response to risk. There was a time that I thought purchasing insurance was the best way to manage risk, and worked closely with my customers to make sure we had the right coverages.

In 1998, I undertook the study of risk management, which ultimately led me to become a Certified Risk Manager and Trainer. It was during this time that I learned insurance only addresses hazard risks, which as a category represents one-fourth of the risks faced by businesses today.

Additionally, hazard risks are negative, with nothing to be gained – the only outcome is loss, and there is no added value. This bothered me greatly because I felt like I was only helping my customers with risks limited to those that could be responded to with insurance products, but not really addressing the bigger issues they were faced with.

WHY BUSINESSES LOSE VALUE

While significant, hazard risks only represent 25% of the business risks faced by an organization. Further, surveys show that these types of risks are the least likely to have a negative impact on an organization's value.

It is interesting to note that three independent surveys conducted on the reasons for business failures and declining stock prices all had the same conclusion. The figure below displays the results of one of the surveys conducted by Mercer MMC. The leading cause was strategic, followed by operational and financial risks. Hazard risks, which attract all of the attention of risk managers and insurance professionals, were never cited, even though it was one of the survey choices.

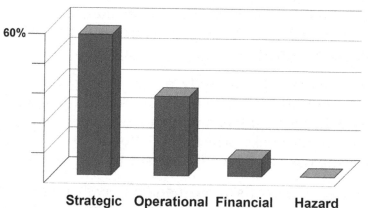

When Companies Lose Value – Which Risk is Greatest?

Strategic, operational and financial risks have a greater potential to adversely impact the organizations bottom line, and they are not insurable. Their impact shows up in sales, productivity, and financial results.

From a management perspective, it also became quite clear that there was confusion about the meaning of the word "risk", not to mention how to manage it. While there were lots of checklists for hazard risks, there was no systematic process being used to identify and manage all the other risks that can have far greater impact on an organization.

Ed Kempkey

Another lesson learned was after I became a certified trainer. At this point I was becoming somewhat of an expert on the subject of risk management and began speaking its language. I could go into great detail about terms and definitions as well as principles and frameworks and how to design and implement them. That was great for conversing with other risk managers or passing exams to become certified, but it was nonsense to the average person.

As the saying goes, we learn from our mistakes, and I certainly made enough of them early on in my efforts to teach risk management. The good news is what the experience has taught me – to be more practical than academic and to put it into a systematic process that is easier to follow.

I wrote this book as my contribution to the education of busy executives on the subject of risk management. Hopefully it will provide you with new insight on risk and how you can use it to improve performance in your organization.

WHY YOU SHOULD READ THIS BOOK

This book is for busy executives who want to improve organizational performance by implementing a structured approach to managing risk. Modern risk management is a team effort, therefore, some critical positions that will benefit from this book include:

- The CEO, who must align the company, internally and externally, with the strategic vision;

- The CFO, who typically has the responsibility for protecting the company against adverse financial results from catastrophic losses;

- The COO, who is responsible for ensuring that business operations are efficient and effective;

- Human Resource Professionals, who are charged with the overall responsibility for implementing strategies and policies relating to the management of individuals;

- The Safety Officer, who is responsible for monitoring and assessing hazardous and unsafe situations and developing measures to assure personnel safety; and

- All other managers who play an important role in achieving your organization's objectives.

Not only can these individuals benefit from the information in this book, they are the very same people who should be part of the process. Modern risk management is a team effort as opposed to the traditional approach, and has evolved significantly over the past two decades.

This book is for you if:

- You would like to promote teamwork and break down silos within the organization

- You would like to establish a reliable basis for decision making and planning

- You would like to increase the likelihood of achieving your organization's objectives

- You would like to avoid being blindsided by the rapidly changing world of business

From my personal experience as a trainer and facilitator, I can tell you that by applying what I will be teaching you:

- Your team will have a deep understanding of what your organization seeks to achieve, as well as a realistic view of the challenges and opportunities it faces.

- Individuals will take ownership for action plans

- You will improve operational effectiveness and efficiency by being able to focus on what matters while encouraging proactive management with measurable results.

Ed Kempkey

In this book, we are going to cover:

- Exactly what it means to manage uncertainty as opposed to risk

- Why managing uncertainty is critical to your success

- The difference between goals and objectives and the various categories of objectives you will want to consider.

- How to efficiently acquire accurate knowledge about the internal and external environment in which your organization seeks to achieve its objectives

- How to assess risks to uncover those most important to achieving your objectives.

- And, most important, how you and your team can leverage this knowledge to make better informed decision that allow you to anticipate threats to the achievement of your objectives and identify opportunities to exploit for a competitive advantage

TABLE OF CONTENTS

ENDORSEMENTS AND ACCOLADES..iii

WHY I WROTE THIS BOOK?..vii

WHY YOU SHOULD READ THIS BOOK...xi

INTRODUCTION...1

CHAPTER 1. ARTICULATE 9

CHAPTER 2. REFLECT..25

CHAPTER 3. ANTICIPATE..39

CHAPTER 4. FOCUS..51

CHAPTER 5. RESPOND..65

CHAPTER 6. SUMMARY..71

ABOUT THE AUTHOR 87

PRODUCTS BY ED KEMPKEY 89

RISK ASSESSMENT WORKSHOP 91

INVITE ED TO SPEAK AT YOUR EVENT! 95

NOTES 97

INTRODUCTION

> *"There are known knowns; there are things we know we know. We also know there are known unknowns; that is to say we know there are some things we do not know. But there are also unknown unknowns – the ones we don't know we don't know.*
>
> **– Donald Rumsfeld, US defense secretary, 2001-06**

Organizations face complexity in distributed operations, relationships, increased regulatory oversight, and litigation burdens. Uncertainty grows right along with business complexity. When risk is considered as the effect of uncertainty on objectives, all efforts to reduce that uncertainty will, therefore, increase the likelihood that the organization will achieve its objectives.

Uncertainty stems from either not having enough information, or the wrong information, to be used in decision-making or planning. When fully integrated into the management and direction of the organization, risk management is just one aspect of management and is just one more tool available to mangers besides tools for operations, finance, planning, human resources, and so forth.

The challenge lies in how we see and respond to risk. This book presents information that will change your perception of risk in order to understand the upside and the many opportunities it can present.

It also provides a roadmap for implementing a systematic process to anticipate and respond to events that may positively or negatively affect your organization's objectives.

To understand the meaning of uncertainty, let's start with the definition of the word "risk". Look it up in any English dictionary and you will see it defined as:

risk

A *chance* or *probability* of loss, injury, or harm.

Games of chance date back to ancient times. The earliest-known form of gambling was a kind of dice game played with what was known as an astragalus, or knuckle-bone. This early ancestor of today's dice was a squarish bone taken from the ankles of sheep or deer. Astragali have surfaced in archeological digs in many parts of the world. Egyptian tomb paintings picture games played with astragali dating from 3500 BC, and Greek vases show young men tossing the bones into a circle. So, games of chance, or gambling, have been part of society for a long time[i].

In fact, probability theory evolved in the seventeenth century based upon mathematical efforts to predict the outcome of a game of chance.

Chance relies on knowing the odds: these are the mainstay of a casino. Imagine a casino not knowing the odds of bets placed on the spin of a roulette wheel. They would not know if, over a large number of bets, the house would win. Knowing the odds allows them to manage the risk without losing money.

Probability relies on knowing the statistics. These are the mainstay of the insurance industry. Imagine an insurance company not having the statistics on automobile accidents. They would not know how much premium to charge in order to pay the claims. Knowing the statistics allows them to manage the risk and make a profit.

Chance and probability rely on odds and statistics. As we have seen, these are the mainstay of casinos and insurance companies. Most businesses, however, operate in a world of uncertainty.

In his book The Failure of Risk Management, author Douglas Hubbard makes the distinction between risk and uncertainty by asking these three questions:

Before the flip of a coin, would you be uncertain of the outcome?

What is the chance the outcome will be tails?

Assuming you are not betting anything on the flip or depending on the flip in any other way, do you have risk in the coin toss?

The answer to the first question of course is yes – the coin has not yet been flipped so the outcome is unknown. Based upon averages, the answer to the second question is there is a 50/50 chance the outcome will be tails. As to the final question, if you have nothing to gain or lose, then you have no risk in the coin toss.

One may have uncertainty without risk, but not risk without uncertainty. The measures for each are quite different in that uncertainty uses a set of possibilities, while risk requires probabilities[ii].

CERTAINTY IS AN ILLUSION

Imagine living in a world of certainty. You would know in advance what schools you would be attending, who would be your friends (and enemies), your career, who you would marry, the names of your kids, grandkids, and on and on. How boring, not to mention downright scary.

The reality is we don't live in a world of certainty (thank goodness), yet as humans we sometimes make decisions under the illusion of certainty, believing that something is certain when it is not. This can be the result of experts and politicians presenting us with information backed up by facts and statistics which are nothing more that predictions and best guesses.

As Ben Franklin said, *"In this world nothing can be said to be certain, except death and taxes."*

The world of certainty is very small indeed – especially when compared to the world of risk and uncertainty.

DECISION MAKING

According to academic research, an adult makes somewhere between 23,000 and 35,000 decisions a day. Many of these decisions are made subconsciously. According to researchers at Cornell University, we make 226.7 decisions each day on just food alone.

Some decisions are relatively insignificant, such as what to have for breakfast or what clothes to wear, and are typically made on an individual basis requiring little thought. Others are more important, requiring a much more refined analysis

Ed Kempkey

and quite often involving group consensus in order to decide on the appropriate course of action.

Historically, an organization's risk management program was transactional in nature with a focus on pure risks. It was typically limited to the purchase of insurance in order to transfer risk whenever possible. The individual(s) responsible operated in a silo, with a limited amount of information being shared with other managers, departments, etc., and consequently was a "bottom-up" process coming from a defensive position.

Modern risk management, now referred to as Enterprise Risk Management, focuses on speculative risks by identifying threats and opportunities while allowing the organization to optimize performance. Those old silos should be broken down, with the various areas of the organization freely collaborating on the efforts and generously sharing information. It is a "top-down" process coming from an offensive position.

So, what's to prevent an organization in moving from a defensive to an offensive position? Besides strong leadership, I believe there are two obstacles that must be overcome to make the transition:

1. Little or no training has been provided on decision making and some of the problems of human nature that affect our ability to make good decisions.

2. A systematic, reliable, and repeatable decision-making process is not used to identify, analyze and evaluate risk in order to make the best decisions on how to respond.

That is why I created the Managing Uncertainty System, a structured series of five conversations you and your team engage in to ultimately make the best-informed decisions that support the achievement of your organization's objectives. And, like most systematic processes, it assures consistent and reliable results.

THE MANAGING UNCERTAINTY SYSTEM

· ·

"If you can't describe what you are doing as a process, you don't know what you're doing."

- W. Edwards Deming

· · · · · · · · · · · · ·

The Managing Uncertainty System is based upon an international risk management standard that is recognized as a national risk management standard in 73 countries, including the United States. Referred to as ISO 31000 Risk Management – Principles and guidelines, it was developed to be used by any public, private, or community enterprise, association, group or individual. It can be applied to a wide range of activities, including strategies and decisions, operations, processes, functions, projects, products, services and assets.

The Managing Uncertainty System builds upon ISO 31000 by specifically focusing on objectives, addressing uncertainty, emphasizing the importance of identifying opportunities, and incorporating a host of proven planning and management tools such as SWOT Analysis, Environmental Scanning, and Management by Objective (MBO).

There are five components to the continuous Managing Uncertainty System. They are:

ATRICULATE – to clearly define your objectives, including the desired outcome and how it will be measured.

REFLECT – to understand the internal and external environment in which your organization seeks to achieve its objectives.

ANTICIPATE – to identify events that might create, enhance, degrade, delay, or prevent the achievement of your organization's objectives.

FOCUS – to analyze and evaluate threats and opportunities to comprehend their nature and magnitude in order to set priorities.

RESPOND – to decide on one or more options for implementing the best action plans to provide or modify controls.

A CONSULTATIVE TEAM APPROACH

The Managing Uncertainty System is best developed in a group setting over a series of brainstorming sessions, or what I refer to as conversations. Participants should be briefed on each step ahead of time, then an individual takes a facilitator's role in conducting the session.

A consultative team approach may:

— ensure that the interests of stakeholders are understood and considered;

— help ensure that risks are adequately identified;

— bring different areas of expertise together for analyzing risks;

— ensure that different views are appropriately considered when evaluating risks;

— secure endorsement and support for a treatment plan;

— enhance appropriate change management during the process; and

— develop an appropriate external and internal communication and consultation plan.

· ·

"If we get the right people on the bus, the right people in the right seats, and the wrong people off the bus, then we'll figure out how to take it someplace great"

- Jim Collins – Good to Great

· · · · · · · · · · · · · · · · · ·

CHAPTER 1

ARTICULATE

Managing Uncertainty Conversation One: Clearly define your objectives, including the desired outcome and how it will be measured.

• •

Alice: *"Would you tell me, please, which way I ought to go from here?"*

The Cheshire Cat: *"That depends a good deal on where you want to go from here?"*

Alice: *"I don't much care where."*

The Cheshire Cat: *"Then it doesn't matter which way you go."*

- Lewis Carroll, Alice in Wonderland

• •

I asked the CEO about his organization's objectives, to which he responded with the following:

1. To be a world class destination.

2. To produce a quality product.

3. To have a productive workforce.

Then I inquired about the length of time for achieving these and how they would be measured, to which he did not have an answer. The CEO had shared the organization's goals with me, but not the objectives. After a discussion about the difference between the two, he said that he needed to work on this and would get back to me.

OVERVIEW

Enterprise Risk Management (ERM) looks at the upside of risk and the many opportunities it can present. It is tied to strategic objectives, and is a coordinated approach that looks at all risk departments.

There are several ERM frameworks, each of which supports the risk management process for decision making in the organization. The frameworks typically describe an approach for identifying, analyzing, evaluating, and responding to events that might enhance or degrade the achievement of an organization's objectives, though little attention is given to defining those objectives.

The Managing Uncertainty System is based on an ERM framework; however, it starts with articulating the organization's objectives, including the desired outcomes and how they will be measured. By doing so it provides the information that allows the other steps in the process to occur, thereby assuring the value and validity of the System.

DEFINITION OF RISK

The Managing Uncertainty System is based on a definition of the word "risk" that comes from an international risk management standard known as ISO 31000 Risk Management Principles and Guidelines. The definition is:

"effect of uncertainty on objectives"

A closer look at this definition reveals its underlying power to both protect AND create value for an organization.

First, an effect is a deviation from the expected – positive and/or negative, so risk can have an upside and/or a downside. You don't get what you want only with the negatives; it's the positive side of risk that equals opportunities.

Second, uncertainty is the state, even partial, of deficiency of information related to, understanding or knowledge of an event, its consequences or likelihood. Good decision-making starts with the right information.

Third, objectives can have different aspects, such as profitability and growth, productivity, brand, reputation, employee morale and development, and physical resources. They can also apply at different levels, such as strategic and operational.

By the very nature of this definition the Managing Uncertainty System is objective-centric, and without clearly stated objectives we cannot comprehend potential threats and opportunities toward their achievement. That is why the first step in the system, Articulate, is to clearly define your organization's objectives. The problem lies in confusion about the meaning of objectives and how to find and set them.

Let's start by looking at the big picture to put this into perspective. Organizations typically have a vision, goals, objectives, and key performance indicators.

VISION

The vision is typically addressed in the mission statement. Historically, mission statements have been focused internally for management, however, there is research that indicates an external focus from a customer's perspective can be far more effective.

Without an effective mission statement, a firm's short-term actions may be counterproductive to long-term interests. As a first step in strategic planning, a mission statement provides direction for all subsequent activities, including communication with perhaps the most important constituency, customers[iii].

GOAL

A goal is a broad primary outcome. It is the Big Picture where we hope that our efforts will ultimately bring us. Goals tend to be long on direction, and short on specific tactics.

OBJECTIVE

A goal is where you want to be, and objectives are the steps taken to reach the goal. Objectives define strategies or implementation steps to attain the identified goals. Unlike goals, objectives are SMART – they must be: Specific, Measurable, Actionable, Relevant, and Time-bound.

Unless results can be appraised objectively, there will be no results, there will only be activity, which is costs. To produce results, it is necessary to know what results are desirable and be able to determine whether the desired results are actually being achieved[iv].

GOALS VS. OBJECTIVES – WHAT'S THE DIFFERENCE?

Goals and objectives are separate but related – they both involve forward motion, but knowing the difference can help us to use both in a constructive way to get us from where we are to where we want to go.

	Goals	Objectives
Definition	Something which you try to achieve.	A specific result that a person or system aims to achieve within a time frame and with available resources.
Time frame	Usually long-term.	A series of smaller steps, often along the way to achieving a long-term goal.
Magnitude	Typically involves life-changing outcomes, like retiring, buying a home, or making a major career change.	Usually a near-term target of a larger expected outcome, such as passing a course as part of completing a degree program.

	Goals	Objectives
Outcome of immediate action	Actions tend to advance progress in a very general sense; there is often awareness that there are several ways to reach a goal, so specific outcomes aren't necessary.	Very specific and measurable, a target is established and victory is declared only when the target is hit.
Purpose of action	A goal is often characterized as a change of direction that will ultimately lead to a desired outcome.	Objectives tend to be actions aimed at accomplishing a certain task.
Example	"I want to retire by age 50."	"In order to reach my goal of retiring at age 50, I need to save $20,000 by the end of this year."
Hierarchy	Goals tend to control objectives; a change in a goal could eliminate one or more objectives, or add new ones.	An objective can modify a goal, but will seldom change it in a fundamental way, even if the objective isn't reached.

STRATEGIC OBJECTIVES

Strategic objectives are measurable, long term organizational goals that help to convert a mission statement from a broad vision into more specific plans and projects. In general, they are externally focused and (according to the management guru Peter Drucker) fall into eight major classifications:

1. Market standing: desired share of the present and new markets;

2. Innovation: development of new goods and services and of skills and methods required to achieve them.

3. Human resources: selection and development of employees;

4. Financial resources: identification of the sources of capital and their use;

5. Physical resource: equipment and facilities and their use;

6. Productivity: efficient use of the resource relative to the output;

7. Social responsibility: awareness and responsiveness to the effects on the wider community of stakeholders;

8. Profit requirements: achievement of measurable financial wellbeing and growth.

Strategic objectives are typically set by top management, followed by obtaining an understanding and agreement within the organization in order for individual managers to describe how their goals, priorities, and strategies can support those of the organization.

Strategic objective examples

Market standing

- Increase the market share by seven percent over the next year.

Innovation

- Develop technological capability to introduce two new products in the next three years.

Human resources

- Maintain employee turnover rate below ten percent for next six months.

Financial resources

- Increase 15 percent the working cash required in each of three banks by year-end.

Physical resources

- Remodel tasting room by May 1st.

Productivity

- Increase revenue per employee by 10%.

Social responsibility

- Sponsor a fundraising event for a local community non-profit organization this year.

Profit requirements

- Increase gross revenue by 5% over last year while maintaining current level of costs.

Results are obtained by exploiting opportunities, not by solving problems. All one can hope to get by solving a problem is to restore normality. All one can hope, at best, is to eliminate a restriction on the capacity of the business to obtain results. The results themselves must come from the exploitation of opportunities[v].

OPERATIONAL OBJECTIVES

Operational objectives (also known as tactical objectives) are measurable short-term goals that assist an organization in achieving its strategic or long-term goals. While closely related to strategic objectives, they differ in that they focus more on "how" than "what." Operational objectives are usually set by middle managers for the next six to twelve months.

Operational objective examples

Human resources department

- Complete within three months an attitude survey of labor-management relations among all employees.

- Complete planning, organization, and installation of an employee development plan for use at the start of next year.

- Implement safety training to be conducted and documented in all departments on a monthly basis.

Sales department

- Meet or exceed quarterly sales target of $(xx).

- Obtain at least (xx) new customers per month.

- Increase the average total amount of each transaction by $(xx).

Marketing department

- Increase sales revenues of a new product 15 percent within 12 months by concentrating existing expense levels of promotion in New England.

- Secure 100 percent distribution in markets D, E, and F of District 3.

- Increase occupancy ratio in hotel rooms from a yearly mean of 65 to 85 percent while maintaining rate structure.

- Complete training program A for all district representatives to assure readiness for distributing product Y at the first of the year.

Finance department

- Achieve an average age of accounts receivable not to exceed 25 days.

- Reduce current debt to tangible net worth position to 35 percent.

HOW MANY OBJECTIVES

The number of objectives to pursue during a coming period varies from company to company. The number of objectives most suitable will be unique to each company because each business differs in the type and number of improvements that must be made within a period of time.

According to the *Pareto effect*, named after the Italian economist Vilfredo Pareto, it is uneconomical to devote the same amount of time and attention to the inconsequential that one devotes to the critical. The practice of managing by objectives forces a manager to sort, select, and concentrate on the critical few as opposed to the trivial many.

One method for sorting these two categories, based on the Pareto principle, is called the M.B.O. Rule for Focus. This rule is described as follows:

1. List all the demands that face a manager.

2. Arrange the list in order of importance.

3. Select the top 20 percent as the critical few.

4. Identify the remaining 80 percent as the trivial many.

5. Spend most of your effort on the critical few.

Thus, objectives can be set giving top priority to vital considerations, leaving matters of lesser importance to be dealt with later. The M.B.O. Rule for Focus helps reverse the trend toward dilution of effort and satisfies completely one of the basic principles of managing by objectives: *The greater the focus and concentration on the results one wants to achieve on a time scale, the greater the likelihood of achieving them[vi].*

KEY PERFORMANCE INDICATORS

A **Key Performance Indicator (KPI)** is a measurable value that demonstrates how effectively a company is achieving key business objectives. Organizations use KPIs at multiple levels to evaluate their success at reaching targets. High-level KPIs may focus on the overall performance of the enterprise, while low-level KPIs may focus on processes in departments such as sales, marketing, or a call center.

KPI examples

Human resources department

- Average revenue per employee (or FTE).

- Average overtime hours per person.

- Percentage of new hire retention after certain period (e.g. 12 months). Number of new hires that still work for the company versus the total number of hires.

Sales department

- Percentage of client/customer facing employees.

- Total sales for a given period divided by the number of customers or transactions for the same period.

- Percentage of customers that are satisfied.

Marketing department

- Percentage of sales relative to the size of the market (market share %).

- Conversion rate of email-generated online traffic.

- Percentage of leads generated via social media.

Finance department

- Average production costs of items produced within measurement period.

- The deviation of the planned budget (cost) is the difference in costs between the planned baseline against the actual budget. (Deviation of planned budget)

- A company's average collection period (accounts receivable, days).

OBJECTIVE REGISTER

Before we go any further, now is a good time to introduce the objective register. An objective register is a tool commonly used in risk management. It acts as a central repository for listing objectives and the associated risks identified by the organization and, for each risk, includes information such as risk event description, level of risk, risk response, detailed action plans and so forth.

I use an Excel spreadsheet that is broken down into four main sections: Articulate; Anticipate; Focus and; Respond.

Here are the columns I use under each of these sections.

Articulate

- Objective
- Desired outcome
- Measures

Anticipate

- Risk event description

Focus

- Consequences
- Likelihood
- Effectiveness of current controls
- Gap summary
- Risk impact
- Risk tolerance
- Risk priority
- Risk financing

Respond

- Risk owner
- Workflow
- Action plan
- Due date
- Progress update

As we go through the rest of this book, you will learn more about why we use the objective register and how to enter the information gained from each of your conversations

SUMMARY

Articulating your objectives is the critical first step in the Managing Uncertainty System. It provides the information that allows the other steps of the process to occur, and if not done thoroughly and competently it will affect the value and validity of the rest of the process. It therefore involves the following:

- Understanding the difference between goals and objectives.

- Developing and communicating strategic objectives.

- Deciding on operational objectives that support the strategic or long-term goals.

- Determining the number of objectives to pursue during a coming period.

- Focusing on opportunities.

MANAGING UNCERTAINTY IN YOUR ORGANIZATION - ARTICULATE

- Decide who will be responsible for developing strategic, operational, and financial objectives.

- Define the strategic, operational, and financial objectives, the desired outcomes, and how they will be measured.

- Once you have articulated your objectives, enter them into a spreadsheet under a column labeled Objectives.

- Name the spreadsheet "Objective Register" and save it.

To learn more about how to clearly define your organization's objectives, visit **www.RiskSkillsCenter.com**.

CHAPTER 2

REFLECT

Managing Uncertainty Conversation Two: Understand the internal and external environment in which your organization seeks to achieve its objectives.

• •

"There are three methods to gaining wisdom. The first is reflection, which is the highest. The second is imitation, which is the easiest. The third is experience, which is the bitterest."

- Confucius

• • • • • • • •

After explaining the **Reflect** step in the process, I opened up the conversation with the seasoned management team. Initially there was silence, then one person commented on an external factor that could be a source of uncertainty for their organization. Then another chimed in with further insight. Two hours later the team had uncovered twenty internal and external factors that were critical to their success.

Later the CFO commented to me that this was the first time he felt the whole team was on the same page and talking the same language. I thanked him for the feedback.

OVERVIEW

The Managing Uncertainty System is a decision-making process that helps organizations make informed choices, prioritize actions, and distinguish among alternative courses of action. The inputs to the process are based on information sources such as historical data, experience, stakeholder feedback, observation, forecasts, and expert judgement.

A key aim of the **Reflect** step in the Managing Uncertainty System is to understand external influences in order to respond in ways that will ensure the organization's survival and success. It is used to evaluate an organization's strengths and weaknesses in response to external threats and opportunities.

The process of understanding the match between external influences and internal responses assists in adjusting organizational structure and strategic plans that are designed to be more effective and flexible to a changing environment.

Reflect provides the information that allows the other steps in the process to occur. Like **Articulate**, if this step is not done thoroughly and competently it will affect the value and validity of the rest of the process.

To accomplish this step, we use a couple of familiar strategic planning tools: Environmental Scanning and SWOT Analysis.

ENVIRONMENTAL SCANNING

Environmental scanning is the internal communication of external information about issues that may potentially influence an organization's decision-making process.

Environmental scanning focuses on the identification of emerging issues, situations, and potential pitfalls that may affect an organization's future. The information gathered, including the events, trends, and relationships that are external to an organization, is provided to key managers within the organization and is used to guide management in future plans. It is also used to evaluate an organization's strengths and weaknesses in response to external threats and opportunities. In essence, environmental scanning is a method for identifying, collecting, and translating information about external influences into useful plans and decisions .

One approach for understanding the external environment is **PESTLE** analysis. The six environmental factors of the **PESTLE** analysis are the following:

POLITICAL ENVIRONMENT

The entire political environment includes government actions which affect the operations of an organization. These actions may be on a local, regional, national or international level, and may also include goods and services which the government aims to provide or be provided, and those that the government does not want to be provided. Political instability can influence the business and the duration of time that business or organization is profitable.

- Taxation policy
- Labor laws
- Environmental laws
- Trade restrictions
- Governmental stability
- Unemployment policy

ECONOMIC ENVIRONMENT

Economic factors greatly affect how businesses operate and make decisions. For example, interest rates affect a firm's cost of capital and, therefore, to what extent a business grows and expands. Exchange rates can affect the costs of exporting goods and the supply and price of imported goods in an economy. Other factors include all the variables that impact how the consumer spends their money and the power of that purchase, such as when during a recession people tend to spend less and save more.

- Interest rate
- Inflation rate
- Growth in spending power
- Exchange rate

- Recession or boom
- Customer liquidations
- Rate of people in a pensionable age
- Unemployment

SOCIO-CULTURAL ENVIRONMENT

Social factors include cultural aspects and health consciousness, population growth rate, age distribution, and career attitudes. High trends in social factors affect the demand for an organization's products or services, and how that organization operates. Organizations look at the cultural characteristics of the society and consider all values and customs that are often associated with the culture while they market their products and services.

- Values
- Beliefs

- Language
- Religion

- Education
- Literacy
- Lifestyle

- Consumer preferences (cars, fashion, where and what to eat, etc.)

TECHNOLOGICAL ENVIRONMENT

Changes in technology affect how an organization will do business. A business may have to dramatically change their operating strategy as a result of changes in the technological environment. The internet has made information available to the consumer to easily compare current prices of a product or service with the price of the competitors of the same product or service. The internet has also created more opportunity to market the products or services an organization offers.

- Internet
- E-commerce
- Social Media

- Electronic Media
- Research and Development
- Cyber security

LEGAL ENVIRONMENT

The legal environment includes current or potential laws in various categories that impact business decisions and activities. Preparing for negative effects of a new law is one example of planning for a changing legal environment. New regulations are expensive in terms of compliance. Laws and regulations will influence the way in which an organization will market or sell its products and services.

- Employment law
- Health and safety
- Product safety
- Product labeling

- Labor laws
- Cyber law
- Consumer law

ENVIRONMENTAL FACTORS

Environmental factors include ecological and environmental aspects such as weather, climate, and climate change, which may especially affect industries such as tourism, farming, and insurance. Furthermore, growing awareness of the potential impacts of climate change is affecting how companies operate and the products they offer, both creating new markets and diminishing or destroying existing ones.

- Competitive advantage
- Waste disposal
- Energy consumption

- Pollution
- Raw materials
- Recyclable products

Other external factors from the various offshoots of PESTLE include:

NATURAL AND COMPETITIVE ENVIRONMENT

A competitive environment is the dynamic external system in which a business competes and functions.

- Direct competitors

- Indirect competitors who offer products or services that can be substituted for one another

RELATIONSHIPS WITH AND PERCEPTIONS AND VALUES OF EXTERNAL STAKEHOLDERS

This includes a person or organization that can affect or be affected by a decision or activity.

- Customers
- Suppliers
- Vendors
- Community at large

EXTERNAL INFORMATION SOURCES

- Personal contacts
- Radio, television, internet
- Journals/magazines
- Professional colleagues
- Books
- Newspapers
- Customers
- Professional conferences/meetings
- Commercial databases

SWOT ANALYSIS

SWOT analysis (alternatively **SWOT matrix**) is an acronym for *strengths*, *weaknesses*, *opportunities*, and *threats* and is a structured planning method that evaluates those four elements of an organization. It is used to evaluate an organization's strengths and weaknesses in response to external threats and opportunities.

By definition, Opportunities and Threats are considered to be external factors over which you have essentially no control.

Strengths and Weaknesses are the internal factors within an organization.

SWOT Analysis framework:

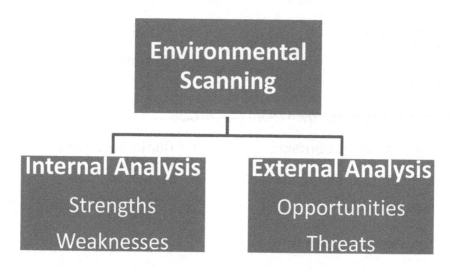

An overview of the four factors (Strengths, Weaknesses, Opportunities, and Threats) is given below.

Strengths - Strengths are the qualities that enable us to accomplish the organization's mission. These are the basis on which continued success can be made and continued/ sustained. Strengths can be either tangible or intangible. These are what you are well-versed in or what you have expertise in, the traits and qualities your employees possess (individually and as a team), and the distinct features that give your organization its consistency. Strengths are the beneficial aspects of the organization or the capabilities of an organization, which includes human competencies, process capabilities, financial resources, products and services, customer goodwill, and brand loyalty. Examples of organizational strengths are huge financial resources, broad product line, no debt, committed employees, etc.

Weaknesses - Weaknesses are the qualities that prevent us from accomplishing our mission and achieving our full potential. These weaknesses deteriorate influences on the organizational success and growth. Weaknesses are the factors which do not meet the standards we feel they should meet. Weaknesses in an organization may be depreciating machinery, insufficient research and development facilities, narrow product range, poor decision-making, etc. Weaknesses are controllable: they must be minimized and eliminated. For instance, to overcome obsolete machinery, new machinery can be purchased. Other examples of organizational weaknesses are huge debts, high employee turnover, complex decision-making process, narrow product range, large wastage of raw materials, etc.

Opportunities - Opportunities are presented by the environment within which our organization operates. These arise when an organization can take benefit of conditions in its environment to plan and execute strategies that enable it to become more profitable. Organizations can gain competitive advantage by making use of opportunities. Organizations should be careful and recognize the opportunities and grasp them whenever they arise. Selecting the targets that will best serve the clients while getting desired results is a difficult task. Opportunities may arise from market, competition, industry/government, and technology. Increasing demand for telecommunications accompanied by deregulation is a great opportunity for new firms to enter the telecom sector and compete with existing firms for revenue.

Threats - Threats arise when conditions in the external environment jeopardize the reliability and profitability of the organization's business. They compound the vulnerability when they relate to the weaknesses. Threats are uncontrollable. When a threat comes, stability and survival can be at stake. Examples of threats are: unrest among employees; ever-changing technology; increasing competition leading to excess capacity, price wars, and reducing industry profits; etc.

INTERNAL ENVIRONMENT

Factors to consider when evaluating the internal environment in which the organization seeks to achieve its objectives include:

GOVERNANCE, ORGANIZATIONAL STRUCTURE, ROLES AND ACCOUNTABILITIES

The framework of rules and practices by which a board of directors ensures accountability, fairness, and transparency in a company's relationship with its stakeholders. Also defines how activities such as task allocation, coordination, and supervision are directed toward the achievement of objectives.

POLICIES, OBJECTIVES, AND THE STRATEGIES THAT ARE IN PLACE TO ACHIEVE THEM

Specific results that a person or system aims to achieve within a time frame and the plan of action or policy designed to achieve them.

CAPABILITIES, UNDERSTOOD IN TERMS OF RESOURCES AND KNOWLEDGE

In other words, capital, time, people, processes, systems, and technologies.

INFORMATION SYSTEMS, INFORMATION FLOWS, AND DECISION-MAKING PROCESSES

Includes both formal and informal.

RELATIONSHIPS WITH AND PERCEPTIONS AND VALUES OF INTERNAL STAKEHOLDERS

This includes a person that can affect, or be affected by, a decision or activity. This would include employees.

THE ORGANIZATION'S CULTURE

The general customs and beliefs of a particular group of people; i.e., the way we do things around here.

STANDARDS, GUIDELINES, AND MODELS ADOPTED BY THE ORGANIZATION

Can be a "best practice", "body of knowledge", "framework", "guidance", "method" etc., in order to promote consistency. Varies significantly by industry.

FORM AND EXTENT OF CONTRACTUAL RELATIONSHIPS

This can include contractual agreements that include hold harmless clauses and insurance requirements with independent contractors and service providers, lessees and renters, bailee, transportation, leased employees, and suppliers.

INTERNAL INFORMATION SOURCES

- Personal contacts
- Internal reports
- Conference papers
- Internal memoranda
- Committees/meetings
- Sales staff
- Other managers
- Other employees
- Internal databases

SUMMARY

Reflecting on your environment is the second step in the Managing Uncertainty System. It helps to understand the internal and external environment in which your organization seeks to achieve its objectives.

After you **Articulate** your objectives, **Reflect** involves the following steps:

- Environmental scanning to understand the external environment, including opportunities and/or threats.

Ed Kempkey

- Review the internal environment to identify factors that could be a source of uncertainty.

- Conduct SWOT analysis to evaluate the organization's strengths and weaknesses in response to external threats and opportunities.

- Revised analysis may mean the objectives need to be changed.

SWOT Analyses are often arranged as a 2 by 2 matrix with the list of strengths and weaknesses in the first two boxes in the first row and the list of opportunities and threats in the second row. By arranging the analysis in this fashion, the lists are separated into internal factors that can affect a project on the first row and external factors on the second row. In addition, the first column consists of the positive factors (strengths and opportunities) and the second column consists of negative actors (weaknesses and threats.). This method provides a simple framework to keep lists organized and conceptualize how the lists are related[viii].

	Positive	Negative
Internal	Strengths 1._____ 1._____ 1._____	Weaknesses 1._____ 1._____ 1._____
External	Opportunities 1._____ 1._____ 1._____	Threats 1._____ 1._____ 1._____

MANAGING UNCERTAINTY IN YOUR ORGANIZATION - REFLECT

- With your team, brainstorm your external environment, including the eight factors that could be a source of uncertainty for your organization, and state each as either a threat or opportunity.

- Brainstorm your internal environment, including the eight factors that could be a source of uncertainty for your organization, and state them as either a strength or weakness.

- Enter your findings into the matrix and distribute to all participants in preparation for your next conversation, *Anticipate*.

To learn more about understanding the environment in which your organization seeks to achieve its objectives, visit www.RiskSkillsCenter.com.

CHAPTER 3

ANTICIPATE

Managing Uncertainty Conversation Three: Identify events that might create, enhance, degrade, delay, or prevent the achievement of your organization's objectives.

. . . .

"It's tough to make predictions, especially about the future."

- Lawrence Peter ("Yogi") Berra

. . . .

A relatively young management team for a non-profit organization was enthusiastically engaged in the *Anticipate* conversation when one of the participants brought up an event that could have a serious financial impact and prevent them from achieving one of their objectives, which was to build a new facility.

As the conversation continued, what started out as a threat turned into an opportunity, and action plans were made accordingly. This contributed to raising three million dollars in the following six months, putting them over half way to their fund-raising goal.

OVERVIEW

One of the most important steps in the Managing Uncertainty System is to identify risk. So far we have defined risk as the effect of uncertainty on objectives and learned that managing uncertainty is all about making informed decisions to achieve those objectives.

In **Anticipate** we are going to learn about the process of finding, recognizing, and describing risks. Our goal at this stage of the process is to develop a comprehensive list of risks based on those events that might create, enhance, prevent, degrade, accelerate, or delay the achievement of objectives.

To assist in finding risks we can refer to a risk library, which ideally is broken down by external and internal risks. The internal risks are further categorized by strategic, operational, and finance risks. Following are some examples.

Note: these are not risk statements, they are simply a listing of risks for reference purposes.

EXTERNAL RISKS

- Alternate Service Provider
- Use Needs
- Economy
- Financial Markets
- Industry
- Legal
- Natural Hazards
- Catastrophe
- Public relations
- Regulatory
- Sovereign/Political
- Technological Innovation

INTERNAL RISKS

Strategic

- Service Model
- Service Portfolio
- Delivery Channels
- Intellectual Property
- Marketing/Advertising
- Marketplace
- Organization Structure
- Planning
- Product Life Cycle
- Resource Allocation
- Social Responsibility
- Mission

Operational

Process

- Alignment
- Business Interruption
- Capacity
- Change Response
- Compliance
- Cycle Time
- Distribution
- Efficiency
- Health & Safety
- Knowledge Management
- Measurement
- Partnering
- Environmental
- User Satisfaction
- Commitment
- Contract Commitment
- Physical Security
- Service Development
- Service Pricing
- Sourcing
- Strategy Implementation
- Supply Chain
- Transaction Processing
- Third Party Outsourcing

Management Information

- Accounting Information
- Budgeting/Forecasting
- Completeness/Accuracy
- Regulatory Reporting

Human Capital

- Accountability
- Change Readiness
- Communications
- Competence/Skills
- Empowerment
- Leadership
- Hiring/Retention
- Succession Planning
- Performance Incentives
- Training/Development

Technology

- Access
- Availability
- Data Integrity
- E-Commerce
- Infrastructure
- Reliability
- Technological Capacity

Financial

- Collateral
- Concentration
- Credit
- Default
- Funding/Gifts
- Endowment
- Financial Instruments
- Foreign Exchange

- Interest Rates
- Liquidity
- Modeling
- Opportunity Cost

- Contract Counterparty
- Cash Flow
- Commodity

Categorizing helps us to think about the types of risks that might be identified. It also sets the stage for focusing on the areas of risk that may have been agreed to before starting the process.

RISK VS. ISSUE

There is a difference between a risk and an issue. A risk must contain some element of uncertainty, such as likelihood of occurrence or consequences of an event. If there is no uncertainty it is not a risk, rather it is an issue. As an example, if during the past several winters the building's roof has leaked and nothing has been done to repair or replace it, then there is not a risk of water damage to the interior during the upcoming winter as it will leak again. This type of situation should not be stated as a risk because it's an issue – just fix it!

DESCRIBING RISKS

There is a way to describe a risk that helps us in analyzing and assessing it later in the process. A good risk description contains four elements: risk *sources*, *events*, and their *causes* and potential *consequences*.

Following are the definitions of each element from the ISO 31000 Risk management – Principles and guidelines, along with examples.

risk source

Element which alone or in combination has the intrinsic potential to give rise to **risk**.

NOTE: A risk source can be tangible or intangible.

Examples

An example of tangible risk source could be an uncovered hole in the sidewalk.

An intangible risk source could be a lack of training.

event

Occurrence or change of a particular set of circumstances

NOTE 1: An event can be one or more occurrence, and can have several causes.

NOTE 2: An event can consist of something not happening.

Examples

An occurrence example would be an earthquake.

A change in circumstances could be the introduction of new laws and regulations that impact the organization.

consequence

Outcome of an **event** affecting objectives.

NOTE 1: An event can lead to a range of consequences.

NOTE 2: A consequence can be certain or uncertain and can have positive or negative effects on objectives.

Examples

Examples include financial, reputational, and regulatory consequences, each of which can be expressed qualitatively or quantitatively.

causes

While not defined in ISO 31000, the term "causes" is used from a practical standpoint to indicate the root cause of the event. According to Wikipedia, a root cause is an initiating cause of either a condition or a causal chain that leads to an outcome or effect of interest. Commonly, root cause is used to describe the depth in the causal chain where an intervention could reasonably be implemented to improve performance or prevent an undesirable outcome.

THE FIVE WHYS

When trying to state the root cause of an event, we can take a lesson from the process used in incident investigations known as Root Cause Analysis (RCA). While the RCA process helps organizations learn from past performance, it can also serve as a reference for understanding the root cause of a potential event.

The root cause of most risks is a failure in the organization's management system. Management systems include company **S**tandards, **P**olicies and **A**dministrative **C**ontrols (SPAC) that have been established for the purpose of ensuring the desired outcome from a given business operation. And, most importantly, management systems are within our control[ix].

While this is an abbreviated discussion about root causes, you can use these terms as a starting point to develop your risk statements. The trick is to ask why a risk exists until the answer contains a root cause and the consequences for not addressing it.

Here are the seven potential failures of a management system:

1. No SPAC, or issue not addressed in SPAC.

2. SPAC not strict enough.

3. SPAC confusing or contradictory.

4. SPAC incorrect.

5. Unaware of SPAC.

6. SPAC recently changed.

7. SPAC enforcement issue.

When stating the cause of an event, ask why five times to get to the root cause. More times than not you will find it to be one of these SPACs. This will aid you greatly when it comes time to choose the proper risk treatment.

When formulating your risk statements, keep the following rules in mind:

- Ensure the risk has some real bearing on objectives.

- Do not make long statements with more than one risk, don't use "or."

- Risks should be concrete and specific, not "an earthquake occurs."

- Stay with the formula of cause & effect.

- Work back in the chain of cause & effect to find the root cause.

When developing your risk statement, it may be helpful to start with the various components and then string them together into a sentence. Referring to the examples below, you can create a table to enter the risk source, event, root cause, and consequence to begin building your risk statements.

Objective: _____

Risk Source	Event	Root Cause	Consequence
inoperative sprinkler system	building burns down	lack of testing	cannot process for six months

Due to a lack of periodic testing, a failure in the sprinkler system goes undetected and is, therefore, unable to respond to a fire that destroys our facility and impedes our ability to operate for six months.

performance measures	inability to achieve objectives	inconsistent with strategies	miss revenue projections by 20%

Use of performance measures that are inconsistent with our strategies hinders our ability to achieve objectives, resulting in missing revenue projections by 20%.

Objective: _____

Risk Source	Event	Root Cause	Consequence

MANAGING UNCERTAINTY IN YOUR ORGANIZATION - ANTICIPATE

- Brainstorm with your team to identify events that could affect the achievement of your objectives positively or negatively.

- Work together to create risk statements that include source, root cause, and consequences.

- Create a new column in your Objective Register with the heading of Risk.

- Enter your risk statements into the Objective Register next to the objectives on which they have an effect.

If you would like to learn more about how to identify events that could affect the achievement of your objectives, visit www.RiskSkillsCenter.com.

CHAPTER 4

FOCUS

Managing Uncertainty Conversation Four: Analyze and evaluate threats and opportunities to comprehend their nature and magnitude in order to set priorities.

. . . .

It is more important to focus on the consequences of an event than on the probability of an event occurring.

Peter Bernstein

. . . .

During a group *Focus* conversation, the vineyard manager of this premium winery was emphasizing the consequences of losing the water supply at one of their prime vineyard properties, even though he didn't know the likelihood.

While other members of the team initially downplayed the risk, he eventually convinced them to rank it high on the list of action plans that needed to be completed. Six months later the water supply dried up and the plans that were put in place eliminated the consequences.

OVERVIEW

We have now identified risks and learned how to describe them by including risk sources, events, and their causes and potential consequences. The next step in the Managing Uncertainty System is *Focus*, which is a two-part process where we first analyze and then evaluate threats and opportunities to comprehend their nature and magnitude in order to set priorities.

Risk analysis not only provides the basis for risk evaluation, it also prioritizes risks and sets the stage for making decisions about risk treatment, which we will learn about in *Respond*.

RISK ANALYSIS

Consequences can affect property, people, dollars, liability, and reputation. Likelihood, simply stated, is the chance of something happening over a specified period of time. A third element to consider in risk analysis is the effect and reliability of existing controls.

We can measure consequences and likelihood using a scale for each that includes descriptors with a numerical value. The same can be done when measuring the effectiveness of current controls. Examples of rating criteria and associated scales are displayed below.

Consequences are the outcome of an event. The following scales may be used for rating negative consequences, starting with the financial scale.

Scale	Financial
5	Severe or Catastrophic >$
4	Major $ to $
3	Moderate $ to $
2	Slight or Minor $ to $
1	Minimal or Insignificant < $

This scale represents the rating criteria for the reputational consequences of an event. You can modify it to your liking.

Scale	Reputational
5	International headline with dramatic change in all stakeholders' confidence.
4	National headline, two or more stakeholder groups lose confidence.
3	National media coverage, one or more stakeholder groups lose confidence.
2	Local headline, one stakeholder group negatively impacted.
1	Local media coverage with minimal change in stakeholder confidence.

This scale represents the rating criteria for the regulatory consequences of an event. You can modify it to your liking.

Scale	Regulatory
5	Major violations resulting in lawsuits and criminal charges.
4	Serious violations resulting in fines, penalties, and lawsuits.
3	Minor violations resulting in fines and penalties.
2	Regulator requests additional information.
1	Regulator not interested in this issue.

You can create your own scale(s) for positive consequences of an event that may cause gain or benefit.

Likelihood is the chance of something happening in the future. The following is an example for rating likelihood.

Scale	Descriptor
5	Probable 81 - 100%
4	Good Chance 61 – 80%
3	Possible 41 – 60%
2	Somewhat likely 21 – 40%
1	Remote 0 – 20%

PRECAUTIONARY PRINCIPLE

I am unsure about its origin, but the Precautionary Principle reminds us about our limitations in knowledge about the future. It applies to the management of risks where there is a high level of consequences, and likelihood is believed to be close to zero, but not zero. In such cases the risk should be treated even though the effects of the treatment may also be uncertain.

Effectiveness of Controls is the measure that is modifying the risk. Controls include any process, policy, device, practice, or other actions which modify risk.

Scale	Descriptor
5	Potentially over-mitigating this risk.
4	Mitigation committed and adequate.
3	Reasonable mitigation, some minor concerns.
2	Some mitigation planned, but effectiveness uncertain.
1	Mitigation insufficient or non-existent.

RISK ANALYSIS RATING CRITERIA

We can use these criteria to rate the consequences, likelihood and effectiveness of current controls. If you have not done so already, in the consequences scale enter the dollar amounts that reflect the different levels of impact on your organization. Above the likelihood scale, enter the number of years over which the chance of something happening will be considered.

EVALUATING RISK

Now that we have learned how to analyze risk by estimating the level of risk using a combination of consequences and likelihood, we will now use that information to make decisions about which risks need treatment and the priority for treatment implementation.

There are two components to evaluating risk: risk tolerance and risk priority. Risk tolerance is the organization's readiness to bear the risk after risk treatment in order to achieve its objectives.

RISK TOLERANCE

This chart displays a rule set for making decisions about whether to treat risk.

Risk Tolerance	Meaning
Low – Avoid	Avoid the risk in its current state by not continuing with the activity that gives rise to the risk. (Not always feasible.)
Moderate – Treat	Select one or more options for modifying risk, and then implement those options.
High - Accept	Accept the risk as is with no need for modification.

RISK PRIORITY

The second component is priority for treatment, which reflects the urgency for completion of risk treatment plans, and the willingness of the organization to continue to tolerate particular levels of risk (pending completion).

The chart below displays the options for priority of treatment.

Priority for Treatment	Meaning
Ongoing	**Ongoing control as part of general management activities.** Should be planned to treat in keeping with all other priorities as part of general or routine management activities.
Treat within one year	**Treat as soon as practicable, but within one year.** Is acceptable for a limited period of time and should be treated as soon as practicable but within one year.
Treat within three months	**Implement treatment as soon as practicable, but no later than three months.** Is only acceptable if it is not practicable to reduce the level of risk immediately, otherwise reduce the level to medium or low as soon as possible, but within three months.
Implement immediately	**Implement treatment immediately or stop until treated.** Is not permitted unless approved by the Board. Reduce level of risk to high or below immediately, or get permission from the Board to continue at this level.

A WORD ABOUT DECISION MAKING

In 2011 Daniel Kahneman's book *Thinking, Fast and Slow,* which summarizes much of his research on judgement and decision making, was published and became a best seller. Kahneman explains two systems that drive the way we think. System 1 thinking is fast and intuitive, it is the subconscious decision making, while System 2 is slow and deliberate, the conscious decision making.

System 1 operates automatically and quickly, with little or no effort and sense of voluntary control. System 2 allocates attention to the effortful mental activities that demand it, including complex computations[x].

JUDGEMENT UNDER UNCERTAINTY

Many decisions are based on beliefs concerning the likelihood of uncertain events. How do people assess the probability of an uncertain event? According to Kahneman, people rely on a limited number of heuristic (roughly, a rule of thumb) principles that sometimes lead to biases that create errors and overconfidence in our decisions.

The representativeness heuristic is one where people evaluate probabilities by the degree to which one thing is representative of another. He uses an example of describing a person's character and then asking people to assess the probability that based upon the description the person is engaged in a particular occupation form a list of possibilities. People order these occupations by the degree to which there is similarity, the stereotype of the person described. This leads to serious errors because similarity, or representativeness, is not influenced by several factors that should affect judgements of probability.

The availability heuristic is one in which people asses the frequency or probability of an event by the ease with which instances or occurrences can be brought to mind. It is a common experience that the subjective probability of traffic accidents rises temporarily when one sees a car overturned by the side of the road.

Adjustment and anchoring is another heuristic that Kahneman describes as, "People make estimates by starting from an initial value that is adjusted to yield the final answer. The initial value, or starting point, may be suggested by the formulation of the problem, or it may be the result of a partial computation. In either case, adjustments are typically insufficient. That is, different stating points yield different estimates, which are biased toward the initial values." He calls this phenomenon anchoring.

A better understanding of these heuristics and of the biases to which they lead could improve judgements and decisions.

GROUP DYNAMICS

Now that we have reviewed some of the challenges associated with making decisions as individuals, let's look at some of the pitfalls that can make group meetings frustrating and unproductive in the decision-making process.

Author Sam Kaner, in his book "Facilitator's Guide to Participatory Decision-Making", paints a good picture of the types of problems that can arise in group decision- making.

In the book, he depicts the typical flow of group decision-making from left to right in a graphical format. On the left side we have divergent thinking, with the arrows representing different ideas coming from individual group members. Later in the meeting it's not uncommon to see the very same people behaving quite differently, with convergent thinking, as shown by the arrows coming together on the right side.

In real life, the process can get a little messy. The gap in the middle of the chart represents a period of time that is stressful for groups. This can be recognized by people repeating themselves, interrupting others, or even going silent. According to Kaner, sometimes what appears to be chaos is actually a prelude to creativity. This period is a very common aspect of life in groups, and we refer to it as the *Groan Zone.*

He goes on to state, "Sometimes the mere act of acknowledging the existence of the *Groan Zone* can be a significant step for a group to take. Expressing difference is natural and beneficial; getting confused is to be expected; feeling frustrated is par for the course. Building shared understanding is a struggle, not a platitude."

Successful group decision-making requires a group to take advantage of the full range of experience and skills that reside in its membership. If a group truly wants to achieve sustainable agreement, then spending time in the *Groan Zone* is critical. The resolution of a *Groan Zone* will occur when a shared framework of understanding has been built[xi].

GROUPTHINK

Groupthink is a term coined by social psychologist Irving Janis (1972) which he describes as a deteriorated and biased view of facts and circumstances because of group pressures to reach consensus. Groups affected by groupthink ignore alternatives and tend to take irrational actions, failing to fully explore the potential outcomes, including the worst-case scenario.

How can groups make decisions better and faster? What are the classic causes of failure in group decision-making? These are the questions that Dr. Clifford Saunders reflected on due to the dismal product development projects in which he was involved and the shortcomings he observed of group dynamics and the way groups make decisions.

He began to study complexity and a tool to resolve complex situations called interactive management. In 1988, Saunders created software, called *Ballot Resolver*, that would eliminate many of these problems and help groups optimize decision- making. Using wireless keypads, Ballot creates an environment of anonymous voting, thereby eliminating the groupthink bias and ensuring candid discussion on a level playing field. I am a fan of this software and use it in the risk analysis phase when conducting a risk assessment workshop.

SUMMARY

Here are some decision-making tips, as they apply to individuals and groups, based upon the information presented above.

AS AN INDIVIDUAL

Know the difference between certainty, uncertainty, and risk, and the appropriate measures to use with each. With risk, everything, including the probabilities, is known. With uncertainty, not everything is known, and one cannot calculate the best option.

Understand System 1 and System 2 thinking and how we can be fooled by heuristics that can lead to biases and errors in judgment, particularly when making decisions about the likelihood of uncertain events.

The way to block errors that originate in System 1 is simple in principle: recognize the signs that you are in a cognitive minefield, slow down, and ask for reinforcement from System 2.

It is much easier to identify a minefield when you observe others wandering into it than when you are about to do so. Be watchful for one another as an individual approaches this minefield.

AS A GROUP

Recognize the existence of the Groan Zone and understand it is a natural part of the group decision-making process.

Encourage all members to speak up and say what's on their minds. Members will become more courageous in raising difficult issues and will learn how to share their "first-draft" ideas.

Members have to understand and accept the legitimacy of one another's needs and goals. This basic recognition is what allows people to think from each other's point of view, the catalyst for innovative ideas that serve the interests of all parties.

Wisdom emerges from the integration of everybody's perspectives and needs. Learn to take advantage of the truth held not only by the quick, the articulate, and the powerful, but also by those who are shy or who think at a slower pace.

MANAGING UNCERTAINTY IN YOUR ORGANIZATION - FOCUS

- In this session, each participant should anonymously vote and express their honest and candid opinions on the ratings for consequences, likelihood, and effectiveness of controls for the identified risks.

- The votes should then be reviewed, and discussion takes place where there is a need to gain further consensus.

- Once discussed, a re-vote can determine the level of agreement.

- As a group, decide which risks need treatment by referencing the risk tolerance and priority rule sets.

- Create five new columns in your Objective Register spreadsheet:

  - Consequences

  - Likelihood

  - Effectiveness of Controls

- Risk tolerance

- Risk priority

• Enter your ratings/rule sets in each of the appropriate columns.

To learn more about how to set priorities for establishing your action plans, visit www.RiskSkillsCenter.com.

CHAPTER 5

RESPOND

Managing Uncertainty Conversation Five: Decide on one or more options for implementing the best action plans to provide or modify controls.

. . . .

An organization's ability to learn,
and translate that learning into
action rapidly, is the ultimate
competitive advantage."

Jack Welch

. . . .

During the course of a two-day conference at which I was invited to be a speaker, I met the CEO of an organization that had been through my training in the past. His team had really embraced the Managing Uncertainty System, and I was proud of the work they had done.

At the end of my one-hour presentation I opened it up to the audience for questions. The CEO immediately stood up and shared how happy he was using the System in his organization. He then proceeded to say that they got more done in the five months after using the System than they had in the previous five years. At that point there was nothing more for me to add to the conversation – I was glad he was there.

OVERVIEW

The next step in the Managing Uncertainty System is **Respond**, where we will decide on one or more options for implementing the best action plans to provide or modify controls. Controls include any process, policy, device, practice, or other actions which modify risk.

There are seven options from which to choose in modifying risk. They can involve:

AVOIDING THE RISK BY DECIDING NOT TO START OR CONTINUE WITH THE ACTIVITY THAT GIVES RISE TO THE RISK.

This is an informed decision to not perform activities that lead to the possibility of loss. A decision to avoid risk may also mean the possibility of not earning profits, and it should also be noted that it may not relieve exposure to products already in the field, or other past activities.

An example of risk avoidance would be a manufacturer who operates a fleet of trucks to deliver their products. They may decide that the control this provides in establishing their delivery schedule is not worth the liability arising out of operating heavy equipment on the highways.

To mitigate this risk, they may state the following: "Put our product delivery business out to bid with for-hire carriers, and place all company-owned equipment up for sale with a local truck dealership."

TAKING OR INCREASING THE RISK IN ORDER TO PURSUE AN OPPORTUNITY

Opportunity may be defined as an exploitable set of circumstances with uncertain outcome, requiring commitment of resources and involving exposure to risk.

Instead of asking about events that could threaten the achievement of our objectives, ask about opportunities to improve the likelihood of achieving those objectives. It changes the whole conversation.

Effective risk management still requires addressing the threats, but it should be balanced with identifying opportunities. That way it both protects and creates value for the organization, providing a much greater return on the investment.

REMOVING THE RISK SOURCE.

Risk source is an element which alone or in combination has the intrinsic potential to give rise to risk. A source can be tangible or intangible. An example of a tangible risk source could be an uncovered hole in the sidewalk. An intangible risk source could be a lack of training.

CHANGING THE LIKELIHOOD

For those risks that we cannot avoid, we institute programs designed to prevent losses. The term "prevention" implies an action taken to break the sequence of events that leads to a loss or makes the event less likely.

An example of loss prevention is when a business implements a safety program to prevent workplace injuries. The elements can include a written safety policy, defined responsibilities and accountabilities, written programs to address hazards, and training and inspection materials.

CHANGING THE CONSEQUENCES

For those losses that do occur, loss reduction methods are used to reduce the severity and financial impact. These methods may involve pre-loss reduction activities or post-loss reduction activities.

Examples of pre-loss activities would be the development of a disaster recovery plan, including training and periodic testing. Post-loss reduction activities could involve claims management, including prompt claims reporting and incident investigation.

If we were going to mitigate the risk of not having a disaster recovery plan, the following statement would be appropriate in the mitigation column of our risk register: "Create a crisis management committee and develop a business continuity plan."

SHARING THE RISK WITH ANOTHER PARTY OR PARTIES (INCLUDING CONTRACTS AND RISK FINANCING)

Contractual risk transfer typically involves hold harmless, indemnity, and insurance provisions in contracts. Examples where this technique is used include contracts with suppliers, vendors, contractors and service providers (including those servicing your premises), bailees, transportation providers, suppliers, leased employees, and lessees and renters. Of course, proof of insurance should be obtained from these other parties to assure their financial responsibility.

To mitigate the risk using this technique, we might state: "Establish a certificate of insurance program, including minimum insurance requirements, for all suppliers, contractors, etc., and maintain proof of coverage from each on an ongoing basis."

Risk financing is a form of risk treatment involving contingent arrangements for the provision of funds to meet or modify the financial consequences, should they occur. Risk financing options include: *retention* which is the acquisition of funds from within the organization to pay for losses or; *insurance* (when available) purchased from a commercial insurance company.

RETAINING THE RISK BY INFORMED DECISION

This involves the assumption of risk of loss, as through the use of non-insurance, self-insurance, or deductibles. The retention can be intentional (active retention) or, when exposures are not identified, unintentional (passive retention).

Risk treatment options are not necessarily mutually exclusive or appropriate in all circumstances. Keep in mind that typically more than one of these strategies is appropriate, and are quite often are used in combination.

RISK OWNERS

For each of the risks that will have an action plan an individual should be assigned as the risk owner. Risk owners have the accountability and authority to manage risk. It is also important that they have the resources (e.g. human, technology, information, finance, etc.) and the competence (training) to manage a risk.

You may also want to assign action plan owners who, from a practical standpoint, indicate a person to whom a task has been assigned by the risk owner.

MANAGING UNCERTAINTY IN YOUR ORGANIZATION - RESPOND

- Brainstorm with your team in selecting one or more options for modifying each risk.

- Assign risk owners, including action plan owners where appropriate.

- Enter the action plans, including risk owners and due dates, into the Objective Register and distribute a copy to all participants.

To learn more about how to implement the best action plans in response to your organization's risks, visit www.RiskSkillsCenter.com.

CHAPTER 6
SUMMARY

Now that you have read the book, I would like to offer a couple of thoughts so you can continue to get the most out of what was learned.

First, communication and consultation with external and internal stakeholders should take place during all steps of the Managing Uncertainty System. Engaging in dialogue with stakeholders provides information that relates to the existence, nature, significance, evaluation, and acceptability and treatment of risk.

As their views can have a significant impact on the decisions made, the stakeholders' perceptions should be taken into account in the decision-making process.

Second, monitoring and review ensures the organization maintains a current and correct understanding of its risks, and that those risks remain within its risk criteria. Monitoring and review can be valuable for evaluating progress, and also for learning lessons for improvement. Communication and consultation will enhance this learning and provide valuable feedback into the review process.

Both monitoring and review should be a planned part of the Managing Uncertainty System and involve regular checking or surveillance. It can be periodic or ad hoc.

Third is recordkeeping. As you monitor and review your progress, be sure to update your Objective Register accordingly. In order to be traceable, you should copy the spreadsheet, make any changes or notes, and then save it by including the date that it was updated in the document name. For example, the name for a June 19, 2017 updated register would be Objective Register 061917.

PRINCIPLES FOR MANAGING RISK

The ISO 31000 International Standard sets forth eleven principles that organizations should comply with for risk management to be effective. Following are the principles along with my comments on how to put them into practice:

a) Risk management creates and protects value.

Risk management contributes to the demonstrable achievement of objectives and improvement of performance in, for example, human health and safety, security, legal and regulatory compliance, public acceptance, environmental protection, product quality, project management, efficiency in operations, governance, and reputation.

How to put this principle into practice

Risk management should make money, enhance reputation, contribute to public safety, improve sustainability, generally enhance benefits, and reduce harm. To ensure its ongoing effectiveness, management should:

- *Support the introduction of risk management by providing a strong and sustained commitment to the organization, as well as strategic and rigorous planning to achieve commitment at all levels. This can be accomplished by defining and endorsing a risk management policy, and assigning accountabilities and responsibilities at appropriate levels within the organization.*

- *Align risk management objectives with the objectives and strategies of the organization. This can be done by understanding the linkage between risk and drivers of value across the breadth of the business. When viewed as the effect of uncertainty on objectives, risk management can look at both the downside and the upside of risk, and the many opportunities it can present.*

b) Risk management is an integral part of all organizational processes.

Risk management is not a stand-alone activity that is separate from the main activities and processes of the organization. Risk management is part of the responsibilities of management and an integral part of all organizational processes, including strategic planning and all project and change management processes.

How to put this principle into practice

Risk management should be woven into business processes using steps to identify, assess, evaluate, mitigate and monitor risks. The risk management process should become part of, and not separate from, those organizational processes. There should be an organization-wide plan to ensure that the risk management policy is implemented and that risk management is embedded in all of the organization's practices and processes.

c) Risk management is part of decision-making.

Risk management helps decision-makers make informed choices, prioritize actions and distinguish among alternative courses of action.

How to put this principle into practice

All decision making within the organization, whatever the level of importance and significance, should involve the explicit consideration of risks and the application of risk management to some appropriate degree.

Identified risks should be analyzed in order to provide an input to risk evaluation and to make decisions on whether risks need to be treated, and on the most appropriate risk treatment strategies and methods.

Risk evaluation involves comparing the level of risk found during the analysis process with established risk criteria. Decisions should take into account the wider context of the risk and should be made in accordance with legal, regulatory and other requirements.

d) Risk management explicitly addresses uncertainty.

Risk management explicitly takes account of uncertainty, the nature of that uncertainty, and how it can be addressed.

How to put this principle into practice

Risk is defined as the effect of uncertainty on objectives. Uncertainty is the state, even partial, of deficiency of information related to, understanding or knowledge of an event, its consequences, or likelihood.

Following a risk assessment process, risks can be analyzed with varying degrees of detail, depending on the risk, the purpose of the analysis, and the information, data and resources available. Analysis can be qualitative, semi-quantitative or quantitative, or a combination of these, depending on the circumstances.

When properly assessed, one or more options can be selected for modifying the risks and implementing those options. Once implemented, any uncertainty regarding the risks consequences and their likelihood, including the impact on objectives, will be reduced accordingly.

e) Risk management is systematic, structured, and timely.

A systematic, timely and structured approach to risk management contributes to efficiency and to consistent, comparable and reliable results.

How to put this principle into practice

The two main components of an effective risk management plan are a framework and a process.

The framework in an organization supports the risk management process for decision making. It includes creating a risk management policy and assigning accountabilities and responsibilities at appropriate levels within the organization.

The process is comprised of activities that support and assist decision making within the organization. The activities include establishing the context and risk criteria for identifying, analyzing and evaluating risks. A system to monitor and review the controls implemented to modify risk is also created.

While it takes a little time to design and implement, operating within a framework and following a process will produce consistent, reliable and sustainable results that provide an excellent ROI on the investment of resources to establish the plan.

f) Risk management is based on the best available information.

The inputs to the process of managing risk are based on information sources such as historical data, experience, stakeholder feedback, observation, forecasts, and expert judgment. However, decision-makers should inform themselves of, and should take into account, any limitations of the data or modeling used or the possibility of divergence among experts.

How to put this principle into practice

Throughout the process of assessing, treating, and monitoring risk, there should be ongoing communication and consultation with internal and external stakeholders. This includes issues relating to the risk itself, its causes, its consequences, and the measures being taken to treat it.

The best method to accomplish this is to take a team approach to managing risk. This typically includes individuals at the management level who are knowledgeable about the organization. Involving a group of people is best because it encourages participation, enhances the visibility and stature of the process, and provides a broad perspective on the issues.

In addition to internal resources, consideration should be given to including subject matter experts when necessary to help ensure that risks are adequately identified. Communication and consultation should facilitate truthful, accurate and understandable exchanges of information, and support a team effort that taps into the collective wisdom of participants to develop a truly effective plan.

g) **Risk management is tailored.**

Risk management is aligned with the organization's external and internal context and risk profile.

How to put this principle into practice

This principle is based upon two byproducts of the risk management process; establishing the context and preparing a risk profile.

The first step in the process is to establish the context by articulating the organization's objectives and defining the internal and external environment in which the organization seeks to achieve its objectives. The external context may include political, legal, regulatory, financial, technological, economic, natural and competitive environment, whether international, national, regional or local. The internal context refers to organization's culture, processes, structure and strategy.

The second step in the process is risk assessment, which includes identifying, analyzing, and evaluating risks in order to prepare a risk profile. The risk profile gives a significance rating to each risk and provides a tool for prioritizing risk treatment efforts. It documents the key risks to an organization to achieving its stated business objectives, and should be used by the management team for strategic and business planning, resource allocation, and action plans.

Alignment with these two key building blocks assures the organization is on the right track in developing an effective risk management plan.

h) Risk management takes human and cultural factors into account.

Risk management recognizes the capabilities, perceptions, and intentions of external and internal people that can facilitate or hinder achievement of the organization's objectives.

How to put this principle into practice

As pointed out in Principle Seven, the first step in the risk management process is to evaluate and understand the context of the organization and how it relates to the scope of the particular risk management process. This includes the cultural and human factors, both internal and external to the organization.

The process should be aligned with the organization's culture, with the human aspect of the context including, but not limited to:

- *Relationships with, perceptions and values of external stakeholders;*

- *Capabilities and knowledge of people;*

- *The relationships with and perceptions and values of internal stakeholders.*

This points again to Principle Six, where consideration should be given to including subject matter experts when necessary to ensure that different areas of expertise and views are considered when defining risk criteria and in evaluating risks.

i) Risk management is transparent and inclusive.

Appropriate and timely involvement of stakeholders and, in particular, decision- makers at all levels of the organization, ensures that risk management remains relevant and up-to-date. Involvement also allows stakeholders to be properly represented and to have their views taken into account in determining risk criteria.

How to put this principle into practice

Plans for communication and consultation should be developed at an early stage of the risk management process. Those accountable for implementing the risk management process, as well as stakeholders, should be well informed on the basis on which decisions are made, and the reasons why particular actions are required.

All members of an organization should be fully aware of the risks, controls and tasks for which they are accountable. This can be indicated by records of meetings and decisions to show that explicit discussions on risk took place. In addition, it should be possible to see that all components of risk management are represented within key processes for decision making in the organization.

Communication and consultation should facilitate truthful, relevant, accurate and understandable exchanges of information, taking into account confidential and personal integrity aspects.

j) Risk management is dynamic, iterative, and responsive to change.

Risk management continually senses and responds to change. As external and internal events occur, context and knowledge change, monitoring and review of risks takes place, new risks emerge, some change, and others disappear.

How to put this principle into practice

A good management system includes the ability to continuously track and evaluate progress in order to make any necessary adjustments in plans that were made. Both the framework that supports the risk management process, and the process itself, contain an element of monitoring and review.

As respects the framework, monitoring and review should include:

- *Periodically measuring progress against, and deviation from, the risk management plan;*

- *Periodically reviewing whether the risk management framework and policy are still appropriate; and*

- *Reporting on risk and how well the risk management policy is being followed.*

As respects the risk management process, monitoring and review should include:

- *Ensuring that controls are effective and efficient in both design and operation;*

- *Analyzing and learning lessons from events (including near-misses) successes and failures; and*

- *Identifying emerging risks.*

The results of monitoring and review should be recorded and externally and internally reported on as appropriate, and used as input for continual improvement.

k) Risk management facilitates continual improvement of the organization.

Organizations should develop and implement strategies to improve their risk management maturity alongside all other aspects of their organization.

How to put this principle into practice

Based upon Principle Ten, an organization should emphasize continual improvement in risk management through the setting of performance goals, measurement, review and subsequent modification of processes, systems, resources, capability and skills.

This can be indicated by the existence of explicit performance goals against which the organization's and individual manager's performance is measured. The organization's performance can be published and communicated. Normally, there will be at least an annual review of performance and then a revision of processes, and the setting of revised performance objectives for the following period. The risk management performance assessment should be an integral part of the overall organization's performance assessment and measurement system for departments and individuals.

HOW DOES YOUR RISK MANAGEMENT PROGRAM MEASURE UP?

The International Risk Management Standard, ISO 31000, consists of guidelines and principles that are considered by many to be the best practices for managing risk today. To see how your organization measures up, place an X in the appropriate box for each of the ten best practices listed below. You can then determine areas for improvement in order to enhance the efficiency and effectiveness of your risk management program.

Practice	None	Very little	Some	Good	Complete
You demonstrate support for the program in a written policy that is approved by the board and clearly states the organization's objectives for, and commitment to, risk management.					
Roles & responsibilities for managing risks are clearly stated, including how performance will be measured and reported, as well as a commitment to providing the necessary resources.					
Your decisions on risk and the management of risk are made according to established expectations that clarify what is (and what is not) an acceptable risk exposure based upon the organizations capacity to take risk and its objectives.					

You continuously communicate and consult with internal and external stakeholders, including subject matter experts when necessary, to ensure that different areas of expertise and views are considered when evaluating risks.					
You have articulated the organizations objectives and defined the external and internal environment in which the organization seeks to achieve its objectives, including the scope and risk criteria for the risk management process.					
You follow a process that identifies risks based on those events that might create, enhance, prevent, degrade, accelerate or delay the achievement of the organizations business objectives.					
Your current methodology identifies the root causes of the events identified and determines the frequency and severity of the event consequences.					

Ed Kempkey

Your corporate risk profile documents risks that are critical to achieving the organization's business objectives over a specified future period of time, and serves as a management tool for strategic and business planning.					
You are able to minimize the probability, frequency, severity, or unpredictability of loss with risk solutions and action plans via "risk owners" responsible and accountable for risk improvements.					
You continuously track and evaluate progress in order to make any necessary adjustments in the plans that were made, including regular reporting, so the business always has a current view of the risk landscape.					

Measure Key

None - Very little or no compliance with the requirement in any way.

Very Little - Only limited compliance with the requirement. Management supports the intent, but compliance in practice is poor.

Some - Limited compliance with element statement. Certainly agree with the intent, but limited compliance in practice.

Good - Management completely subscribes to the intent, but there is partially complete compliance in practice.

Complete - Absolute compliance with the element statement – in intent and in practice – at all times and in all places.

FINAL THOUGHTS

Any management team can develop its own effective risk management program. All it takes is leadership and five to ten managers willing to work through the process. In preparation, participants should read the appropriate sections in this book to prepare for each conversation in advance. Based upon my experience as a facilitator, here are some tips for efficiently implementing effective risk management:

Meet frequently during the learning phase in order to keep the information fresh and the momentum moving. I would suggest meeting at least once a week, which gives everyone time to prepare for each of the conversations.

Don't try for perfection at the early stages. It takes a while to identify and describe a risk, so do your best and in time and with a little repetition it will come easy. You will also find that in time you will be able to more easily identify opportunities to exploit – especially when dealing with strategic risks.

Benchmark your practices periodically in order to measure your development. Use the ratings for the ten best practices discussed above to help you measure and develop an effective risk management program over time. You may even want to use it to see where you stand now and establish a baseline.

Don't get discouraged. You are learning a new skill that takes time to apply. I have seen management teams struggle for the first 90 days, and in six months it becomes natural. In one year they are in a leadership position based upon the benchmarks.

Share your success. If you have a board, keep them informed with progress reports like updated risk registers and benchmark reports. I have seen where even telling key customers has been well received – they are impressed. And certainly, staff should be included as appropriate.

I have enjoyed writing this book, and sincerely hope it serves you well. If you have any questions please feel free to contact me at ed@riskskillscenter.com.

If you would like Ed to facilitate your organization's five conversations, he can be reached at (707) 738-7977.

ABOUT THE AUTHOR

Ed Kempkey helps management teams implement a strategic process that not only anticipates events that can threaten the achievement of objectives, but also identifies opportunities to exploit for a competitive advantage.

Ed is the founder of Risk Skills Center, which provides an educational resource for mid-size organizations. He is a Certified Risk Manager (CRM), Certified ISO 31000 Trainer, and author of two books on risk management. As a veteran of the industry, Ed observes that most business risks are not covered by insurance, and for those that are covered, the total cost of a loss goes far beyond what is paid by the insurance company.

Large companies have full-time risk managers whose job it is to identify, assess, and mitigate the organization's risks. The challenge faced by most mid-size and smaller organizations is a lack of resources, namely time and talent, to accomplish this. Meanwhile, the evolution of risk management concepts and tools during the past decade has progressed to the point where they can be adopted as a best practice for use by organizations of all sizes.

Recognizing the need, Ed has developed numerous educational resources for small to mid-size organizations. Based upon his many years of helping companies implement effective risk management programs, the range of offerings includes executive coaching on program design, board briefings and training, management and risk oversight committee training, and facilitating risk assessment workshops.

Ed has presented numerous seminars on a variety of risk management topics including safety and health, enterprise risk management, root cause incident investigation, business continuity planning, and human resource related subjects.

Ed has earned the designation CT31000 – Certified ISO 31000 Lead Trainer. This means he has demonstrated knowledge, proficiency, and competence, and the skills and ability to train others about the ISO 31000 International Risk Management Standard. His picture has appeared on the front cover of a national risk management magazine in connection with a story on his work with the wine industry.

Ed is an experienced pilot and enjoys flying for pleasure and business. He holds a commercial pilot's license with multi-engine and instrument ratings. In addition to flying, he enjoys riding his motorcycle on the back roads of the California North Coast.

Located in Napa, California, he can be reached at ed@riskskillscenter.com or by phone at (707) 738-7977.

PRODUCTS BY ED KEMPKEY

THE MANAGING UNCERTAINTY SYSTEM ONLINE COURSE

For the individual in the organization who takes a leadership position to implement an effective risk management program and provide for its ongoing success, this online course will guide you through the process.

This course is comprised of five modules, one for each of the conversations in which you and your team will participate. The information contained in each of the modules will prepare you to take a leadership role in facilitating each of the conversations.

Included are downloadable documents and worksheets that will enable you to brief the participants on each step ahead of time so they can come prepared to the sessions.

DECISION SMART ONLINE TRAINING

This online course is for decision makers in organizations who are trying to cope with the uncertainty associated with relentless change. You will learn:

- Why risk and uncertainty are not the same and how they should be treated differently.

- How to avoid errors when dealing with judgement under uncertainty.

- How to recognize and overcome problems associated with group decision-making.

- How groups can make decisions faster and better.

- How to use an information-filtering process to make the right decisions.

Visit www.RiskSkillsCenter.com for more information.

RISK ASSESSMENT WORKSHOP

A key component of a successful risk management program is establishing a system for accurately assessing the organizations risks. Risk assessments include identifying, analyzing, and evaluating organizations risks in order to decide on the proper treatments for those that are most critical to achieving its objectives. There are numerous ways to assess risks, including interviews, questionnaires, checklists and documentation reviews. While these can be used to supplement the process, the preferred method is a risk assessment workshop.

A workshop format enables participants to both contribute and learn in a natural environment. The result is not only a ranked list of key risks, but a fascinating discussion about the control environment, risk appetite, and individual risk tolerances. As stakeholders walk away from the session their understanding of business operations, objectives, and challenges has expanded and they are equipped with the knowledge and the detailed analysis to make improved decisions.

The average workshop lasts about 3 hours and typically has 5-10 executives, a record keeper, and a facilitator. The facilitator guides the group through a set of risks and the group determines the impact and likelihood of the risks by consensus. To avoid groupthink or the potential bias that one individual can place on the group opinion, voting software is used to enable anonymous assessment of risk in a workshop environment.

In my experience, the benefits of a workshop go far beyond assessing risks.

Learning opportunity: A well-structured workshop allows participants to examine risks from a range of perspectives, and learn from other experts and leaders in the room. Participants will inevitably emerge from the workshop understanding their business better and with heightened awareness of corporate objectives, and the landscape of internal and external risk environments. If the workshop agenda includes discussion of current, committed, and contemplated mitigants, they will also gain a greater understanding of how other parts of the organization are mitigating risk, and how these mitigants might fit together.

Team building: Risk workshops are an excellent tool for promoting team building. A risk workshop provides a "safe" environment to share perspectives and ideas and ensures equal opportunity for participants. It is a great "get to know you" exercise for a recently established management team.

Efficient use of time: Risk workshops can be an effective way for a management team to cover a large amount of ground very quickly. The focus on a defined agenda and use of facilitation techniques and risk management tools ensures that the discussion sticks to the highest-priority issues.

Risk management education: Risk workshops provide a "live" demonstration of risk management techniques and approaches. As such, they are an excellent vehicle for educating participants on the theory and application of risk management to specific business problems.

Continuous improvement: Risk workshops provide the risk manager with an environment for continuously improving the quality of tools and techniques. By repeated exposure and use by manager from a variety of levels and backgrounds, a pro-gram of workshops will effectively validate such tools as risk tolerances and voting guides.

Risk assessment workshops not only serve as the core activity in the risk management process, they also provide a wonderful combination of learning and teambuilding.

To learn more or to schedule a risk assessment workshop for your organization, contact Ed Kempkey at ed@riskskillscenter.com or (707) 738-7977.

INVITE ED TO SPEAK AT YOUR EVENT!

For nearly two decades Ed Kempkey has been educating and helping busy executives implement effective risk management programs that go beyond insurance. With a focus on the upside of risk, he teaches methods that not only anticipate threats to achieving the organization's objective, but also how to identify opportunities to exploit for a competitive advantage.

Ed has been invited to speak at the Boys and Girls Clubs of America, the California CPA Association, Vistage, and many other associations and groups. His easy-going style both informs and inspires audiences while providing the tools and strategies they need to improve performance.

For more information call (707) 738-7977 or email ed@riskskillscenter.com.

ONE LAST THING...

If you enjoyed this book or found it useful I'd be very grateful if you'd post a short review on Amazon. Your support really does make a difference, and I read all the reviews personally so I can get your feedback and make this book even better.

If you'd like to leave a review then all you need to do is click the review link on this book's page on Amazon here:

http://amzn.to/2BDk0V3

Thanks again for your support!

NOTES

i Bernstein, Peter L. *Against the Gods: The Remarkable Story of Risk.* New York, John Wiley & Sons 1998

ii Hubbard, Douglas, *The Failure of Risk Management: Why It's Broken and How to Fix It.* New Jersey, John Wiley & Sons, Inc. 2009

iii David, M. E., David, F. R., & David, F. R. (2014). Mission Statement Theory and Practice: A Content Analysis and New Direction. *International Journal of Business, Marketing, and Decision Sciences Volume 7, Number 1,* 95-110.

iv Drucker, P. F. (1974). *Management: Tasks, Responsibilities, and Practices.* New York: Harper & Row.

v Drucker, P. F. (1986). *Managing for Results.* New York: Harper.

vi Mali, P. (1972). *Managing by Objectives.* New York: John Wiley & Sons, Inc.

vii Albright, K. (2004). Environmental Scanning: Radar for Success. *The Information Management Journal,* May/June 2004, 38-44.

viii Osita, I.C., Onyebuchi, I.R., & Justina, N. (2014). Organization's stability and productivity: the role of SWOT analysis. *International Journal of Innovative and Applied Research, Volume 2, Issue (9), 23-32.*

ix Root Cause Analysis Handbook, Third Edition, ABS Consulting

x Kahneman, Daniel, *Thinking Fast and Slow,* New York, Farrar, Straus and Giroux 2011

[xi] Kaner, Sam, *Facilitator's Guide to Participatory Decision-Making*, San Francisco, Jossey-Bass 2014

ADDITIONAL READING RESOURCES

Albright, K. (2004). Environmental Scanning: Radar for Success. *The Information Management Journal,* May/June 2004, 38-44.

Cerulo, Karen A. *Never Saw it Coming,* Chicago, The University of Chicago Press 2006

Curtin, J. (2009). Values-Exchange Leadership®: Using Management by Objective Performance Appraisals to Improve Performance. Kravis Leadership Institute, *Leadership Review, Fall 2009, (66-97).*

Gigerenzer, Gerd, *Risk Savvy: How to Make Good Decisions,* New York, Penguin Group 2014

Gotteiner, S. (2016). *The OPTIMAL MBO: A Model for Effective Management-by-Objective Implementation. European Accounting and Management Review, Issue 2, (42-56).*

Hacking, Ian, *The Emergence of Probability: A Philosophical Study of Early Ideas about Probability, Induction and Statistical Inference.* New York, Cambridge 1975

Helms, M.M., Nixon, J. (2010). Exploring SWOT analysis – where are we now? A review of academic research from the last decade. *Journal of Strategy and Management,* Vol.3 No.3.

Harris, Jim, *Blindsided.* Oxford, Capstone Publishing Ltd. 2002

Howard, Ronald A. *Foundations of Decision Analysis,* Essex, Pearson Education Limited 2016

Lam, James, Enterprise Risk Management: From Incentives to Controls, New Jersey, John Wiley & Sons 2003

Ed Kempkey

Mali, P. (1972). *Managing by Objectives.* New York: John Wiley & Sons, Inc.

Morrison, J.L. (1992). Environmental Scanning. *The Association for Institutional Research, A primer for new institutional researchers, (86-99).*

Slywotzky, Adrian, *The Upside: The 7 Strategies for Turning Big Threats into Growth Breakthroughs,* New York, Random House 2007

Taleb, Nassim, *The Black Swan: The Impact of the Highly Improbable,* New York, Random House 2007

Weick, Karl E. and Sutcliffe, Kathleen M. *Managing the Unexpected.* San Francisco, Jossey-Bass 2007

ORGANIZATIONS

International Organization for Standardization, www.iso.org

G31000 Global Institute for Risk Management Standards www.g31000.org

RIMS –The Risk Management Society https://www.rims.org

Made in the USA
Columbia, SC
31 January 2018